OXFORD CHRISTMAS MUSIC

JAMES BASSI

CAROL SYMPHONY

For Mixed Choir (SATB),
Mezzo-soprano Solo, and Chamber Orchestra

CHORAL SCORE

OXFORD
UNIVERSITY PRESS

JAMES BASSI
CAROL SYMPHONY

For Mixed Choir (SATB),
Mezzo-soprano Solo, and Chamber Orchestra

Duration: approx. 13 minutes

The orchestration of *Carol Symphony* evolved partly out of practicality. My colleague Johnson Flucker, music director at the Cathedral of St. John the Divine in New York City, commissioned me to write a work that could be performed alongside Handel's *Messiah* (Christmas portion) for a holiday concert at the Cathedral. We agreed that I would score the symphony for "Messiah" orchestra, using no additional players or instruments, with the exception of a few extra percussion instruments. For me, one of the more exciting challenges in composing *Carol Symphony* was to create a lush, contemporary orchestration using limited instrumental forces.

The first movement, "Bells," is a fantasia on a popular Ukranian carol melody, to which I have written my own English lyrics. It is an impressionistic piece, by turns melancholy and vigorous.

The second movement, "Hymn," is a more or less strophic setting of the Irish *Wexford Carol*. In my earlier version for choir and organ, Judy Collins originally sang the solo part. The clarity and directness of her singing serves as a guideline for soloists approaching this piece. It does not warrant a full operatic sound; it is closer to the folk tradition in overall presentation. The singer should simply tell the story. Given the low tessitura of the part, and depending on the acoustics involved, I would recommend amplification of the soloist, to achieve an easy balance with the accompanying forces.

The third movement, "Dance," is a kind of rhythmic theme-and-variations on the English carol "Tomorrow Shall Be My Dancing Day." The tune undergoes a series of transformations, appearing in different meters, and never in its original 6/8 version. An orchestral toccata section precedes the spirited finale.

—*James Bassi*

The full score and set of parts (2ob., bn., 2tpt., perc., str.) for *Carol Symphony* are available on rental from the Publisher. A setting of the second movement, *Wexford Carol*, for mezzo-soprano, SATB, and organ, with optional handbells, is offered for sale (0-19-386576-9).

CAROL SYMPHONY

For Mixed Choir (SATB), Mezzo-soprano Solo, and Chamber Orchestra

James Bassi

I. Bells

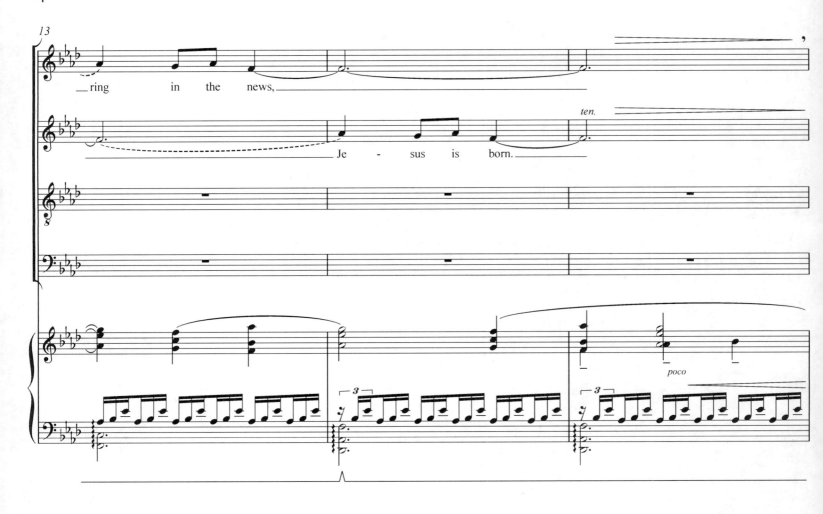

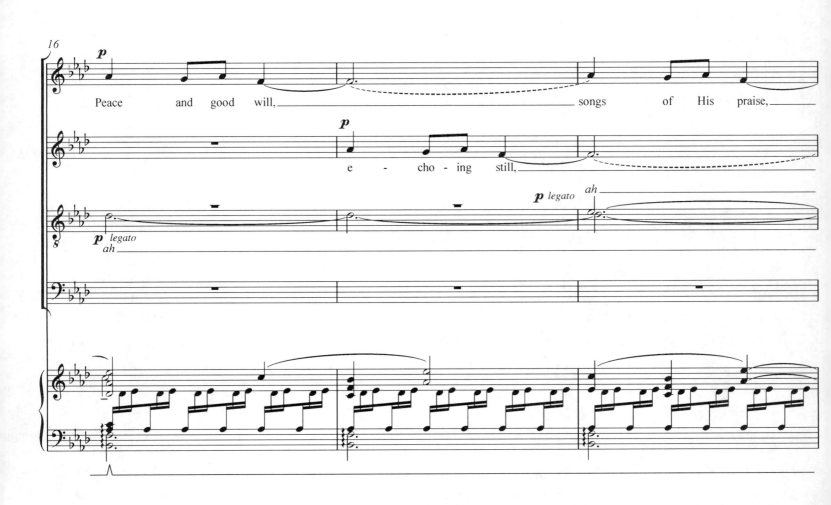

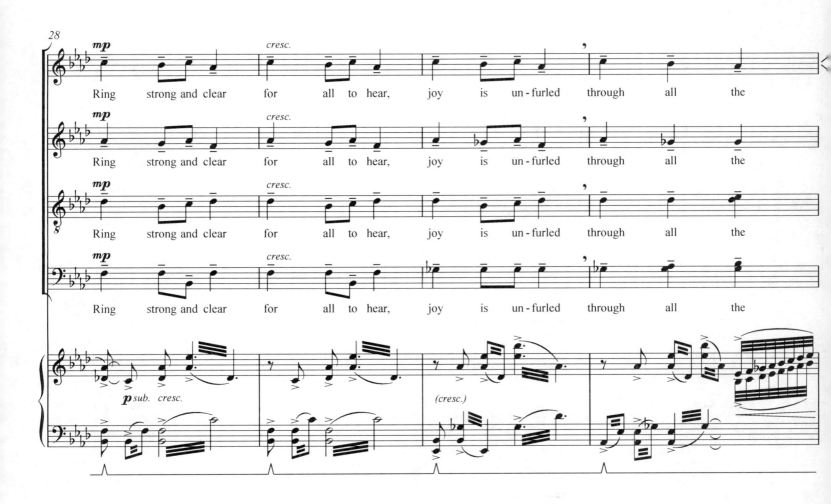

E Allegro, ritmico (♩ = c. 138)

Ring out _____ the bells! _____

F S. 1&2 tutti

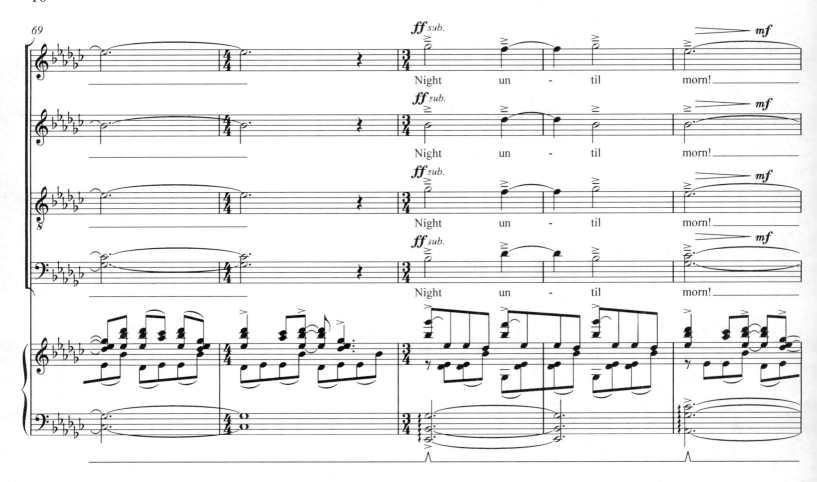

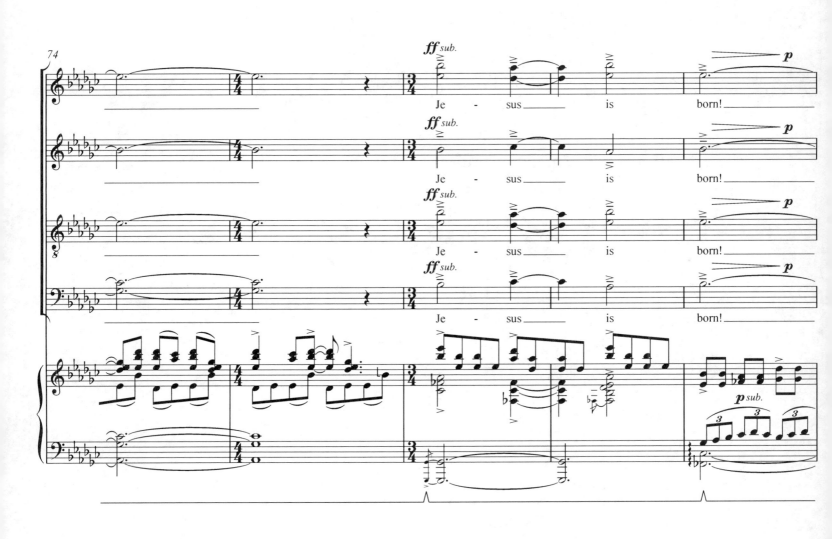

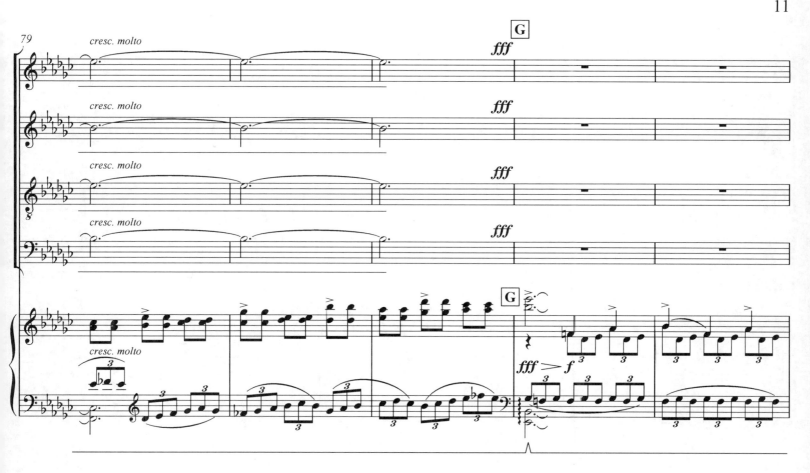

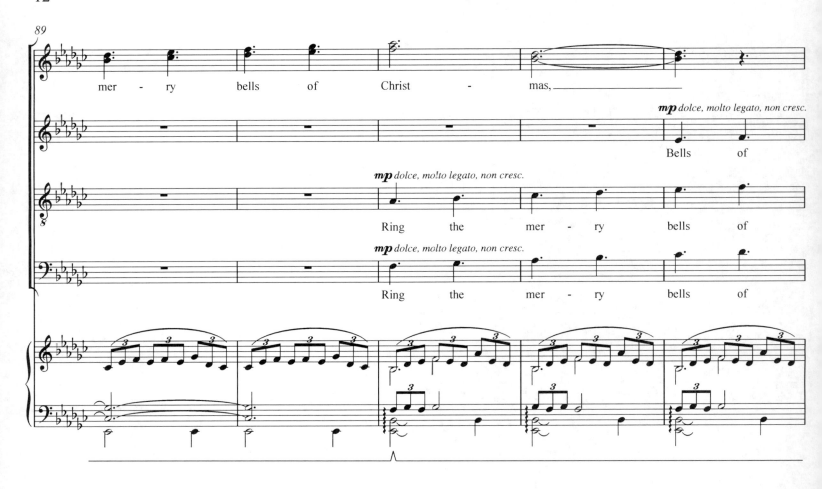

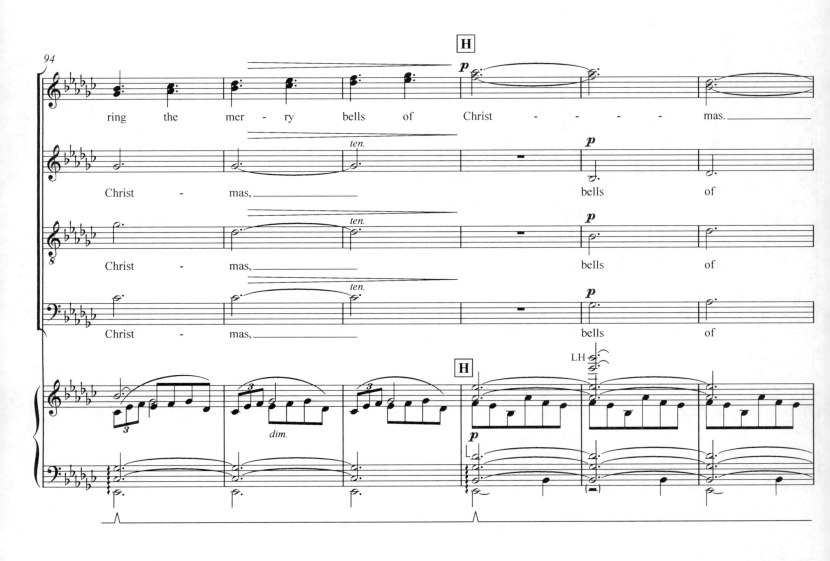

II. Hymn
(Wexford Carol)

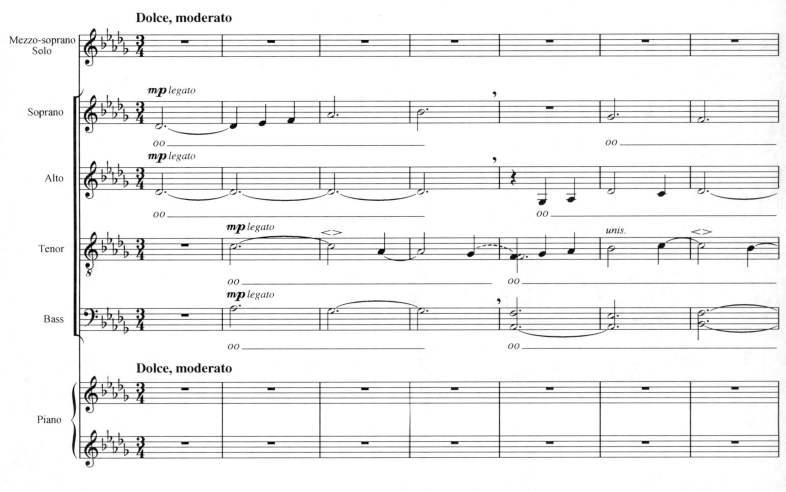

J Calmato, poco meno mosso

What our good God for us has done, in

send - ing his be - lov - ed Son.

III. Dance

32